# REAL LIFE MATH

## solve a

# CRIME

**Wendy Clemson, David Clemson,
Kev Pritchard, and Dr. Allison Jones**

## Ticktock

This library edition published in 2014 by Ticktock
First published in the USA in 2013 by Ticktock,
an imprint of Octopus Publishing Group Ltd

Distributed by Black Rabbit Books
P.O. Box 3263, Mankato, MN 56002

With thanks to our consultants: Jenni Back and Liz Pumfrey from the NRICH Project,
Cambridge University, and to Kerry Johnson, Debra Voege and Lorna Cowan.

Cataloging-in-Publication Data is available from the Library of Congress
ISBN 978 1 78325 192 6

Printed and bound in China

1 3 5 7 9 10 8 6 4 2

### WENDY CLEMSON

Wendy is experienced in working with and for children, and has been writing full-time since 1989. Her publications, which now exceed one hundred, have been written for children and sometimes their parents and teachers. In her many math books, the aim is always to present the reader with challenges that are fun.

### DAVID CLEMSON

David has wide-ranging experience as a writer and educationalist. His publications list is prodigious. In collaboration with Wendy, David has worked on many math books for children. He is fascinated by math and logic puzzles and is eager for the reader to enjoy them, too.

### KEV PRITCHARD

Kev is an experienced crime scene investigator (CSI) with many years experience of examining crime scenes of every type. He is now a senior lecturer in the Department of Forensic and Investigative Science at the University of Central Lancashire, England, where he trains the CSIs, detectives, and forensic scientists of the future.

### DR. ALLISON JONES

Allison is a forensic scientist. Her past experience includes the development of car paint analysis and the analysis of sunscreens. Allison is now a senior lecturer in the Department of Forensic and Investigative Science at the University of Central Lancashire, England, where she teaches the use of analytical techniques in forensic science and the practices involved in the handling and analysis of forensic evidence.

# CONTENTS

## MATH SKILLS COVERED IN THIS BOOK:

### CALCULATIONS:
Throughout this book there are opportunities to practice **addition**, **subtraction**, **multiplication**, and **division** using both mental calculation strategies and pencil and paper methods.

### NUMBERS AND THE NUMBER SYSTEM:
- COMPARING NUMBERS: pg. 14
- DECIMALS: pg. 19
- ESTIMATING: pg. 12
- FRACTIONS: pg. 19

### SOLVING "REAL LIFE" PROBLEMS:
- CODES: pg. 24
- MEASURES: pgs. 10, 14
- MONEY: pg. 6
- TIME: pgs. 10, 16

### HANDLING DATA:
- BAR GRAPHS: pg. 18
- CHARTS: pg. 20
- TALLY CHARTS: pg. 21
- USING TABLES/CHARTS/DIAGRAMS: pgs. 8, 9, 10, 11, 12, 14, 15, 22

### MEASURES:
- AREA: pg. 23
- RELATIONSHIPS BETWEEN UNITS OF MEASUREMENT: pg. 14
- TIME (reading from analog clocks): pg. 17
- USING MEASUREMENTS: pgs. 10, 14, 18
- VOCABULARY (time): pg. 16

### SHAPE AND SPACE:
- 2-D SHAPES: pgs. 6, 27
- COMPASS DIRECTIONS: pg. 26
- GRID COORDINATES: pg. 9
- SYMMETRY: pg. 27

**Supports math standards for ages 10+**

# HOW TO USE THIS BOOK

**M**ath is important in the lives of people everywhere. We use math when we play a game, ride a bike, go shopping – in fact, all the time! Everyone needs to use math at work. You may not realize it, but a detective uses math to solve a crime! With this book you will get the chance to try lots of exciting math activities using real life data and facts about the work of detectives and forensic scientists. Practice your math skills and experience the thrill of what it's really like to solve a crime.

**This exciting math book is very easy to use – check out what's inside!**

Fun-to-read information about crime solving.

## WITNESS STATEMENTS

**S**everal good pieces of **evidence** have been found at the crime scene – the footprints, the broken glass with blood splashes, the single hair, the palm print, and some **fingerprints**! It is not just physical evidence, such as fingerprints, that are collected at a crime scene. Detectives can also collect verbal (spoken) evidence, by taking **statements** from **witnesses**, **victims**, and **suspects**. One of the millionaire's neighbors has given you some interesting information. The neighbor cannot walk very well, and so she spends a lot of time looking out her window. On the day of the burglary, she saw someone running from the mansion's back gate, dressed in black and wearing a ha

## MATH ACTIVITIES

Look for the
**YELLOW CLIPBOARDS.**
You will find real life math activities and questions.

To answer some of the questions, you will need to collect data from a DATA BOX. Sometimes, you will need to collect facts and data from the text or from charts and diagrams.

Be prepared! You will need a pen or pencil and a notebook to figure out the answers.

### DETECTIVE WORK

The person the neighbor saw was wearing white sneakers and glasses and was taller than the mansion's gate. The gate is – *64 inches high.*

Everyone who lives or works at the mansion, or who was seen near the house on the day of the burglary, has been interviewed. The suspects were asked if they ever wear glasses, if they own a pair of white sneakers, and how tall they are. Their answers have been put in the DATA BOX. Use the data to answer these questions:

1) How many people never wear glasses?
2) Who does not own white sneakers?
3) Which two suspects are the same height?
4) What is the difference in height between the tallest person and the shortest person?
5) Which of the suspects could the neighbor have seen running from the mansion's back gate?

(Don't forget to write the names of your suspects into your notebook.)

*(You will find a TIP to help you with these questions on page 28.)*

### CSI FACT

**CSIs** are trained in a special interview technique called *cognitive interviewing.* They interview the victims of crimes, and then use special "E-FIT" computer software to produce a likeness of the **perpetrator's** face.

Fun-to-read facts about forensic science and the work of detectives.

## DATA BOX

If you see one of these boxes, there will be important data inside that will help you with the math activities.

## MATH ACTIVITIES

Feeling confident? Try these extra **CHALLENGE QUESTIONS.**

# IF YOU NEED HELP...

## TIPS FOR MATH SUCCESS

On pages 28–29 you will find lots of tips to help you with your math work.

## ANSWERS

Turn to pages 30–31 to check your answers.
(Try all the activities and questions before you take a look at the answers.)

## GLOSSARY

On page 32 there is a glossary of detective words and a glossary of math words. The glossary words appear **in bold** in the text.

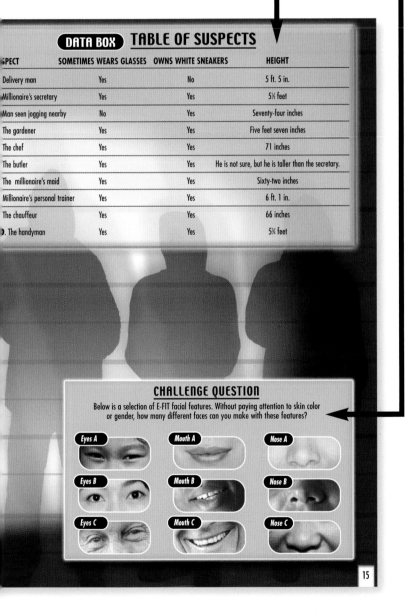

**DATA BOX** **TABLE OF SUSPECTS**

| SPECT | SOMETIMES WEARS GLASSES | OWNS WHITE SNEAKERS | HEIGHT |
|---|---|---|---|
| Delivery man | Yes | No | 5 ft. 5 in. |
| Millionaire's secretary | Yes | Yes | 5½ feet |
| Man seen jogging nearby | No | Yes | Seventy-four inches |
| The gardener | Yes | Yes | Five feet seven inches |
| The chef | Yes | Yes | 71 inches |
| The butler | Yes | Yes | He is not sure, but he is taller than the secretary. |
| The millionaire's maid | Yes | Yes | Sixty-two inches |
| Millionaire's personal trainer | Yes | Yes | 6 ft. 1 in. |
| The chauffeur | Yes | Yes | 66 inches |
| ). The handyman | Yes | Yes | 5¾ feet |

## CHALLENGE QUESTION

Below is a selection of E-FIT facial features. Without paying attention to skin color or gender, how many different faces can you make with these features?

Eyes A    Mouth A    Nose A

Eyes B    Mouth B    Nose B

Eyes C    Mouth C    Nose C

15

# 911 – THERE HAS BEEN A BURGLARY!

There has been a burglary at the luxury mansion of a millionaire. The millionaire is away on his yacht, and one of his servants has just discovered the crime. The first police officer to arrive at the scene of a crime in response to a 911 call is called the first-responding officer. This officer secures the scene using police tape, which stops people from walking around the crime scene and possibly destroying **evidence**. Next, the officer calls for any assistance needed – for example, a detective and a **crime scene investigator (CSI)**, as well as an ambulance if someone is injured. Today, you are the detective on duty. Grab your notebook and pencil – it is time to get to work.

## DETECTIVE WORK

The safe is empty! All that the thief has left behind are some paper bands from the bundles of banknotes and some of the empty boxes where the millionaire's jewels were kept.

1) In the DATA BOX you will see the bands that came off the missing money. How much was stolen?

Look at the jewel boxes in the DATA BOX.
The missing gems have left holes in the boxes.
The holes have made five shapes.
*For example, there is a square in the sapphires box.*
2) Which of the boxes contain these shapes?
   a) **Equilateral triangle**   b) **Isoceles triangle**
   c) **Hexagon**                d) **Octagon**

Here are the values given to each of the gemstones:
   • Diamond $100   • Sapphire $85   • Ruby $65

3) What is the value of the stolen gems in each of the jewel boxes:
   Box A) Sapphires?
   Box B) Rubies?
   Box C) Diamonds?

*(You will find TIPS to help you with these questions on page 28.)*

## POLICE WORK FACT

The first-responding officer starts off the police investigation. On arrival at the scene, the officer thinks through some important questions. What has happened here? What evidence has been left behind? Is there any evidence that needs protection from the weather? Where is the **perpetrator** now?

## CRIME SCENE FACT

Depending on the type of crime, different personnel will be called to a crime scene. These can include CSIs and **forensic scientists**, police dog handlers and their dogs (when searching for drugs), and fire and explosives officers for arson (fire) investigations.

# WHAT HAS BEEN STOLEN FROM THE SAFE?

**Box A: Sapphires**

**Box B: Rubies**

**Box C: Diamonds**

$1,000    $1,000    $1,000    $500

$500    $500    $500    $500

**Money bands**

## CHALLENGE QUESTION

The thief has dropped the numbers that helped him or her crack the code to the safe. The code is made up of **products** that appear in the 12 times table.

Find the products and then write them down in order, starting with the smallest number.

What is the code to the safe?

17    29    24    13    12

8    36    72    58    97

6    48    11    5    54    26

*(You will find a TIP to help you with this question on page 28.)*

7

# THE CRIME SCENE

The burglary took place in the mansion's dining room, where the safe is hidden behind a family portrait. This means the dining room is now a crime scene and will be examined by an expert **crime scene investigator (CSI)**. The CSI is in charge of the crime scene and is responsible for protecting the scene and everything in it. CSIs have the power to stop other people entering a crime scene, even the most senior police officers. CSIs must be meticulous and pay attention to every detail – they cannot make mistakes. The examination of the crime scene is the most important stage in a criminal investigation. Missing a piece of **evidence** could ruin a case!

## CSI WORK

A CSI needs to *process a crime scene*. This means taking photographs of the crime scene from all angles. The CSI also makes a sketch of the crime scene to show the positions of doors and windows and the distances between all the objects in the room.

Look at the photograph of the dining room in the millionaire's mansion. On page 9, you will see four different sketches of the dining room.

*Which sketch matches the photograph of the dining room?*

(You will find a TIP to help you with this question on page 28.)

## EXAMINING A CRIME SCENE FACTS

- First the CSI checks the scene cordon (the police tape) and adjusts the area of the crime scene if he or she feels it should be bigger or smaller.

- The CSI then takes photographs and makes sketches. If someone needs to check something about the crime scene at a later date, they can then use these pictures. The photographs will also be used as evidence in court.

- Next, the CSI searches the scene for evidence. Each item of evidence is given a unique number made up from the CSI's initials and then a consecutive number; so if CSI Joe Bloggs has found his third piece of evidence at a scene, it would be numbered JB3.

## CSI FACT

All personnel entering a crime scene must wear protective clothing to stop hairs and fibers from their own clothes **contaminating** the scene. While working at a crime scene, the CSI wears hooded coveralls, a face mask, gloves, and shoe covers.

SKETCH PLAN A

SKETCH PLAN B

The red crosses show where you are standing. This will help you find the sketch that matches the photograph.

Millionaire's dining room

SKETCH PLAN C

SKETCH PLAN D

# CHALLENGE QUESTIONS

The CSI makes a "crime scene report" listing all the items recovered (found) at the scene. Now that you have figured out the sketch that shows the room, you can use the grid on the sketch to find some clues!

Here are some pieces of evidence and their coordinates on the grid:

- Muddy footprints (5,2)   • Splashes of blood on broken glass (6,2)   • **Fingerprints** (3,4) (0,4) (5,5)
- A palm print (2,4)   • A single hair (5,4)

a) Which clue is outside the French windows?   b) Which clues are in the safe?
c) Where were fingerprints found?   d) Which clues were left just inside the French windows?
e) Where was a palm print found?

*(You will find TIPS to help you with these questions on page 28.)*

# EXAMINING THE CRIME SCENE

**W**hen searching a crime scene, there are two very important areas to examine: the point of entry, or *ingress*, and the point of exit, or *egress*. At the mansion you are examining the French windows in the dining room. It looks as though the **perpetrator** used the French windows to come in and out of the house. There are muddy footprints just inside the French windows, and you have found some fragments of glass just outside the windows, where one of the panes has been broken. You see there are some splashes of blood on the glass. The thief must have smashed the glass and been cut when breaking in!

## DETECTIVE WORK

The perpetrator must have escaped through the mansion's gardens, and so the police are searching the grounds. Find out how long it would take someone to run between some of the features in the grounds of the mansion.

If it takes about a minute to run 200 yards, how long does it take to run:

1) From the main gate to the mansion?
2) From the main gate to the garage and stables?
3) From the summerhouse to the boathouse via the greenhouse?
4) If the distance from the back gate to the turnoff for the boathouse is 300 yards, how long does it take to run from the boathouse to the mansion?
5) How much longer does it take to run from the tennis court to the summerhouse than from the tennis court to the mansion?

*(You will find TIPS to help you with these questions on page 28.)*

## THE MILLIONAIRE'S ESTATE

**DOCK**

**MAIN GATE**

**GATEHOUSE**

## CSI FACT

If a crime scene is inside a building, the **CSI** searches from the point of entry to the property — for example, through the garden, towards the main focus of the crime, such as a safe, and then back to the point of exit.

## CHALLENGE QUESTION

Here is a diagram of places to visit in the mansion grounds.

How many different routes can you find to visit each of the places once, starting and finishing at the main gate?

# RECOVERING EVIDENCE

The crime scene at the mansion has been sketched and photographed. Now the **CSI** must find and recover (collect) any forensic **evidence**. Any piece of evidence that is found has to be securely packaged and then labelled with details of where it was found, when, and by whom. The most common types of evidence found at crime scenes are blood, hairs, fibers (from clothes), glass fragments, tiny chips or slivers of paint, soil and plant material, footwear and footwear marks, **fingerprints**, items of clothing, and documents. When all the forensic evidence is recovered, the CSI examines the crime scene for fingerprints.

## CSI WORK

You have already shown that you are good at assessing a crime scene.

Now see how good you are at looking for details.
First, study the picture of dining room A. Then look at dining room B. List all the things that are different in your notebook.
How many differences can you find?

*(You will find a TIP to help you with this activity on page 28.)*

## CHALLENGE QUESTION

Fingerprints are usually *latent*, meaning they cannot be seen in normal light. CSIs use lots of different techniques to find and enhance the prints (make them visible).
The fingerprint can then be photographed or lifted, using clear, sticky tape.

a) **Estimate** the number of fingerprints that you think are on pages 12 and 13. Write your estimate in your notebook.

b) Now count the fingerprints. How many are there?

*(You will find information about ESTIMATING on page 28.)*

**Recovering the blood splashes**

## CSI FACT

CSIs take *control samples* at a crime scene. For example, if a fingerprint is found, the CSI will try to find prints (or prints will be taken later) from the people who live at the house. These **elimination prints** will then be compared to the fingerprint found at the crime scene. This helps to show if the fingerprint belongs to the **perpetrator**, or to one of the residents.

## CSI FACT

Close-up photographs are taken of each piece of evidence before it is recovered. Tool and footwear marks are photographed next to a scale (a bit like a ruler), so that the photographs can be enlarged to life-size back at the lab.

**Dining room A**

**Dining room B**

## RECOVERING EVIDENCE FACTS

### BLOOD
Pools of blood are recovered using a pipette. Blood that has soaked into a surface is allowed to dry, and then the material is packaged up. Dry blood is removed using a razor blade or a cotton swab moistened with water.

### HAIR
Hairs are normally large enough to see. The CSI can pick them up using tweezers or lift them using a special sticky tape.

### FINGERPRINTS
CSIs shine special lights on fingerprints, brush them with powders, or use chemicals that turn the fingerprint a color that can be seen. All these methods help the fingerprint show up against its background. Sometimes CSIs will remove something large, such as a door, and take it back to the lab for enhancement if they believe there could be a fingerprint on it.

### GLASS
When pieces of glass are recovered, they must be put in plastic containers or boxes. They should not be put in plastic bags, which the glass could cut through, or in glass containers. The glass container could break, mixing with the evidence glass.

# WITNESS STATEMENTS

**S**everal good pieces of **evidence** have been found at the crime scene — the footprints, the broken glass with blood splashes, the single hair, the palm print, and some **fingerprints**! It is not just physical evidence, such as fingerprints, that are collected at a crime scene. Detectives can also collect verbal (spoken) evidence, by taking **statements** from **witnesses**, **victims**, and **suspects**. One of the millionaire's neighbors has given you some interesting information. The neighbor cannot walk very well, and so she spends a lot of time looking out her window. On the day of the burglary, she saw someone running from the mansion's back gate, dressed in black and wearing a hat!

## DETECTIVE WORK

The person the neighbor saw was wearing white sneakers and glasses and was taller than the mansion's gate. The gate is — *64 inches* high.

Everyone who lives or works at the mansion, or who was seen near the house on the day of the burglary, has been interviewed. The suspects were asked if they ever wear glasses, if they own a pair of white sneakers, and how tall they are.
Their answers have been put in the DATA BOX.
Use the data to answer these questions:

1) How many people never wear glasses?
2) Who does not own white sneakers?
3) Which two suspects are the same height?
4) What is the difference in height between the tallest person and the shortest person?
5) Which of the suspects could the neighbor have seen running from the mansion's back gate?

(Don't forget to write the names of your suspects into your notebook.)

*(You will find a TIP to help you with these questions on page 28.)*

## CSI FACT

**CSIs** are trained in a special interview technique called *cognitive interviewing*. They interview the victims of crimes, and then use special "E-FIT" computer software to produce a likeness of the **perpetrator's** face.

## **DATA BOX** TABLE OF SUSPECTS

| SUSPECT | SOMETIMES WEARS GLASSES | OWNS WHITE SNEAKERS | HEIGHT |
| --- | --- | --- | --- |
| **1**. Delivery man | Yes | No | 5 ft. 5 in. |
| **2**. Millionaire's secretary | Yes | Yes | 5½ feet |
| **3**. Man seen jogging nearby | No | Yes | Seventy-four inches |
| **4**. The gardener | Yes | Yes | Five feet seven inches |
| **5**. The chef | Yes | Yes | 71 inches |
| **6**. The butler | Yes | Yes | He is not sure, but he is taller than the secretary. |
| **7**. The millionaire's maid | Yes | Yes | Sixty-two inches |
| **8**. Millionaire's personal trainer | Yes | Yes | 6 ft. 1 in. |
| **9**. The chauffeur | Yes | Yes | 66 inches |
| **10**. The handyman | Yes | Yes | 5¾ feet |

## CHALLENGE QUESTION

Below is a selection of E-FIT facial features. Without paying attention to skin color or gender, how many different faces can you make with these features?

**Eyes A**

**Mouth A**

**Nose A**

**Eyes B**

**Mouth B**

**Nose B**

**Eyes C**

**Mouth C**

**Nose C**

# INTERVIEWING SUSPECTS

he **suspects** have now been narrowed down. There are seven people who could have been the mysterious figure that the neighbor witnessed running from the grounds of the mansion. Do you have the correct seven people written in your notes? The maid has confirmed to you that she discovered the crime. The maid finished dusting in the dining room at 3:40 p.m. and at that time all was well. When she returned at 4:00 p.m. with a vase of fresh flowers for the table, the French windows were swinging open and the safe was empty! Now you need to find out what your suspects were doing at the time the crime was committed.

## DETECTIVE WORK

On these pages you will see the suspects' **statements**. Each of the suspects was asked what they were doing from 2:00 p.m. onwards on the day of the burglary.

All the suspects were busy in the afternoon, but some of them had finished their work by 3:40 p.m.

Read the statements. Who had time to commit the crime?

### SUSPECT STATEMENT: Millionaire's personal trainer

The personal trainer says he was alone in the summerhouse doing yoga for 45 minutes, and then he lifted weights for about three-quarters of an hour. He started at 2:00 p.m.

### SUSPECT STATEMENT: The chef

The chef started making bread at 2:00 p.m. This was his timetable:

- Set out ingredients and make dough — 10 minutes.
- Make soup while the dough rises — 20 minutes.
- Knead dough and allow to rise again — 5 minutes.
- Put dough in oven. Tidy up and wait for bread to bake — 35 minutes.

### SUSPECT STATEMENT: The secretary

The secretary says she was in her office at the gatehouse typing letters. She then went out of the main gate to walk to the village to mail the letters, but she does not know at what time she left because her watch is broken. It takes 40 minutes to walk to the post office.

### SUSPECT STATEMENT:
### The gardener

The gardener was busy all afternoon in the greenhouse taking plant cuttings. He started at 2:00 p.m. and took 8 minutes to plant each cutting. He took 12 cuttings.

### SUSPECT INTERVIEW:
### Handyman

The handyman started painting railings by the main gate at 2:00 p.m. There are 28 railings and each one took five minutes to paint. (You notice he has painted them all.) The handyman says he saw the secretary leave with some letters in her hand as the village clock struck the half-hour. He saw the chauffeur drive in the main gate soon after that.

### SUSPECT INTERVIEW:
### The butler

The butler sat down in the butler's pantry at 2:00 p.m. and wrote out the household tasks for next week. For each day this takes 11 minutes.

## CHALLENGE QUESTION

The chauffeur has just remembered the exact time that she returned to the mansion.

She remembers seeing the church clock in her rearview mirror as she drove into the main gate.
What time did the clock say?

(Remember the clock was reversed because it was being seen in a mirror.)

### SUSPECT STATEMENT:
### The chauffeur

The chauffeur says she started cleaning the car at 2:00 p.m. This took 55 minutes. She then drove into the village to get gas. She thinks this took about 35 minutes.

# ANALYZING CLUES: THE FOOTPRINTS

The pieces of **evidence** collected at the crime scene have now been given to the **forensic scientists** in the laboratory. It is time to see if we can eliminate some more **suspects**. Footwear prints can be as unique as a **fingerprint**. As we walk around in our shoes each day, we wear them down and they become damaged by small stones or bits of glass. This damage is unique – no other shoe will have the same pattern of damage. A footwear mark recovered at a crime scene can be compared with the suspect's shoe to prove that the shoe was at the crime scene. Footwear marks can either be *latent*, meaning they cannot be seen in normal light, or *patent*, meaning they can be seen.

## FORENSIC WORK

The footprints found in the dining room at the mansion are patent. No one was allowed to come in or out of the French windows until the footprints had been photographed and recovered.

The two footprints measured 10½ and 11 inches in length. Look at the **bar graph** to find out what shoe sizes they are.

11 in.

10½ in.

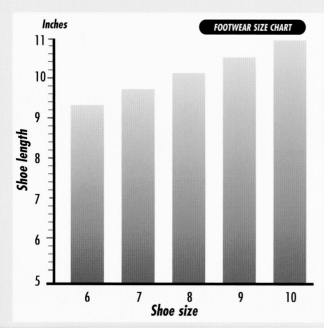

FOOTWEAR SIZE CHART

Inches / Shoe length / Shoe size

In the DATA BOX are the shoe sizes of the remaining suspects. Who could have made the footprints?

*(You will find TIPS to help you with this activity on page 29.)*

### RECOVERING 3-D FOOTWEAR MARKS

A footmark left in mud that has dried (a 3-D, or three-dimensional, mark) can be cast. A plastic frame (like a little fence) is pushed into the ground around the mark. A casting compound is mixed up and poured into the frame and into the footmark. When the cast sets, it can be lifted and transported to the laboratory to be examined.

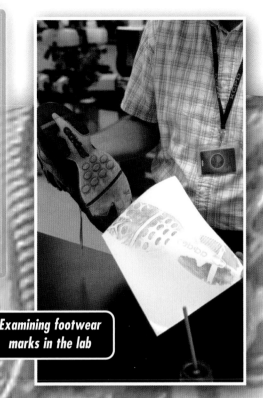

*Examining footwear marks in the lab*

## 2-D FOOTWEAR MARKS

One way to recover marks left on hard surfaces is to use ESLA (electrostatic lifting apparatus). A special plastic sheet is rolled over the print. An electric current is then passed through the sheet. Any dust particles are attracted to the plastic in the shape of the print. Back at the lab, a powerful light is shone over the sheet, and the prints can be seen and photographed.

Sometimes special paper with adhesive or gelatin is used – like large sticky labels. The paper is placed over the mark. After a few minutes, it is lifted and the dust or mud is transferred to the paper in the same size as the original footmark.

## CHALLENGE QUESTIONS

When you buy a pair of shoes or sneakers they have a manufactured sole pattern. These patterns are stored in a computer database. Forensic scientists can use this information to **estimate** the make and model of a shoe.

Study these muddy footprints. The mud on the sneakers fills a **fraction** of the markings on each sole.
a) What fraction of the marking is filled in on each of the four shoes?
b) Convert the answers for shoes B and D to **decimal fractions**.

SHOE A          SHOE B          SHOE C          SHOE D

# ANALYZING CLUES: BLOOD AND HAIR

**W**e are now analyzing the single hair and the blood splashes that were found at the crime scene. The blood has been removed from the glass and is being tested to find out if it is blood type *A, B, AB,* or *O.* All humans have one of these four blood types. The hair has been mounted on a microscope slide and is being examined at 100 times normal magnification. **Forensic scientists** can then tell whether it is a human or animal hair and confirm the color of the hair. By examining the hair tip, scientists can even see if the hair has been cut recently and whether it was cut by scissors or clippers.

## FORENSIC WORK

The blood found at the scene is type B, and the hair found in the safe is brown. We can now eliminate some more **suspects** by comparing their hair color and blood types.

A chart showing the blood and hair information has been drawn up. One person has been put in the chart already. Draw the chart in your notebook and put the other suspects in the correct sections.

| Blood type | Hair color | |
|---|---|---|
| | **Brown** | **Not brown** |
| **Blood type B** | 🧑 | |
| **Not blood type B** | | |

Who could still be the **perpetrator**?

**GARDENER:**
Brown hair / Blood type: B

**CHEF:**
Brown hair / Blood type: A

## BLOOD FACT

For many years doctors tried to transfuse blood from one person to another. This often failed because the blood went lumpy, killing the patient. In 1901, a scientist called Karl Landsteiner discovered that all blood is not the same. Landsteiner and his colleagues discovered there are four types of blood. A blood transfusion will work only if blood of the right type is given to the patient.

# HAIR FACTS

Approximately 100 head hairs fall out of each person every day, and so hair is often found at a crime scene. Hairs from the different areas of the human body look different under a microscope.

A hair is made up of three layers: the CUTICLE (the outer covering), the CORTEX (the inner part), and the MEDULLA (a tube in the center of the cortex). The cuticle is made of colorless scales that overlap, like the tiles on a roof. The shape of the scales can be used to tell human and animal hairs apart. The cortex is important in forensic work because it has pigment granules that give the hair its color.

> **Magnified human hair with cut tip**

**PERSONAL TRAINER:**
Black hair / Blood type: O

**BUTLER:**
Brown hair / Blood type: B

# CHALLENGE QUESTIONS

About two or three weeks after a haircut, hair tips begin to look rounded. The hair found at the crime scene is still square — it has been cut recently!

You are visiting the village hairdresser to check whether any of the brown-haired suspects have had a haircut in the last week. The hairdresser is going to consult her "tally chart" of customers.

| HAIR COLOR | NUMBER OF CUSTOMERS |
|---|---|
| BROWN | ЦЦ ЦЦ ЦЦ |
| BLACK | //// |
| WHITE | ЦЦ /// |
| RED | // |
| BLONDE | ЦЦ // |

While the hairdresser checks, see if you can answer these questions:

a) How many customers did she have?
b) How many of her customers did not have white hair?
c) Six of the customers have dyed hair.
   What **fraction** is that of the total?

*(You will find information about TALLY CHARTS on page 29.)*

# ANALYZING CLUES: FINGERPRINTS

The patterns of ridges that you have on your hands, fingers, and thumbs are unique to you. The ridge patterns form before we are born and they stay the same our whole lives, unless they are damaged by burning or bad scarring. There are sweat pores along the length of the ridges, and so if a finger comes into contact with a suitable surface, a thin, normally invisible, impression is left in sweat. This is a **fingerprint**. It means a particular person was at a crime scene, but it cannot prove when. Fingerprint officers compare prints found at a crime scene with inked fingerprints taken from **suspects**, the **victim**, and other people who were at the scene.

## FORENSIC WORK

If fingerprints match up, the identification is regarded as being *absolute* – the person was definitely at the scene.

Look at these partial fingerprints found in the safe at the millionaire's mansion.

1) Which of the **elimination prints** do they match?

a)

b)

c)

d) e)

### ELIMINATION PRINTS

*Millionaire*

*Butler*

*Gardener*

2) Who is now your main suspect?

**Suspects are fingerprinted at a police station by a fingerprint officer.**

# THERE ARE THREE MAIN CLASSES OF FINGERPRINTS:

**PLAIN ARCH**   **TENTED ARCH**

## ARCHES

Ridges enter from one side and exit from the other. Arches can be subdivided into plain arches and tented arches.

**SPIRAL WHORL**

## WHORLS

A spiral whorl contains at least one ridge that makes a complete 360° turn around the print.

**PLAIN LOOP**

## LOOPS

Loops generally have at least one ridge that starts on one side, extends across the finger, and curves back to the same side.

### Galton's details

As well as working out what class a fingerprint is, there are tiny details on fingerprints known as *Galton's details*. These can all be useful when comparing fingerprints.

*Ridge Ending*

*Lake*

*Bifurcation*

*Independent Ridge*

**The butler's palm area is 23 in.$^2$**

**The gardener's palm area is 21¾ in.$^2$**

## CHALLENGE QUESTIONS

Count the whole squares in this palm print found in the dining room.

Each whole square measures one square quarter-inch, and so you can find the area of the palm print in square inches (in.$^2$).

a) Who does the palm print belong to?

b) Who is now your main suspect? (Write it down!)

c) Find the area of the palm of your hand. What is the difference between your palm area and the gardener's? The butler's?

The investigation is over – who is your main **suspect**? All the **evidence** is pointing towards just one person – the gardener! He had enough time to commit the crime. It could be his footprint in the dining room, his blood on the broken glass, and his hair in the safe. The **fingerprints** found in the safe were definitely the gardener's. You receive a telephone call. The village hairdresser has just confirmed that the gardener had his hair cut last week! It is time to confront your main suspect. You find the gardener in the greenhouse, but he is acting suspiciously and refuses to answer any more questions. You decide to arrest the gardener and take a look around.

## DETECTIVE WORK

Before he was arrested, the gardener was busy piecing together a note. It looks like some sort of code.

Cracking codes is a specialist skill, but in the DATA BOX you will see a grid that will help you to untangle the gardener's secret message.

To use the grid you have to write the number of a row and then the number of a column to make a letter. For example, 15 is *row 1* and *column 5*, which gives the letter **e**. The letter made by 43 is **r**, and 51 is either **u** or **v**. Use the grid to crack the code. What does the gardener's secret message say?

*The gardener is arrested.*

### EVIDENCE FACT

Each piece of evidence gathered in a case must have a *chain of evidence*. This is an unbroken chain of written evidence that tells the story of what has happened to the article, from the moment it was recovered at the crime scene, until it appears in court. Every police officer or scientist who comes into contact with the evidence must keep the chain going. If there are any gaps in the chain, the piece of evidence could be considered unusable in court!

### FORENSICS FACT

Small amounts, or traces, of evidence found at a crime scene help investigators show that there is a link between the crime scene and a suspect. For example, if we can find the gardener's sneakers, we can compare them with the footwear mark found at the scene. Our footprint contains unique details from the sole of the shoe. These unique damage marks can prove that the gardener's shoe was at the scene of the crime.

# CODE CRACKER

|   | 1 | 2 | 3 | 4 | 5 |
|---|---|---|---|---|---|
| 1 | a | b | c | d | e |
| 2 | f | g | h | i | j |
| 3 | k | l | m | n | o |
| 4 | p | q | r | s | t |
| 5 | uv | w | x | y | z |

2235    4535    452315    45431515

4435514523    3521    452315

22431515342335514415

113414    3435434523  52154445

3521    452315    451534342444

1335514345    113414    32353531

2434    452315    23353215

2434    452315    4543513431

## CHALLENGE QUESTION

Try making up your own secret code. You can give each letter a number from 1 to 26, but start with the first letter of your name as number "1."

*(You will find some more information about making up SECRET NUMBER CODES on page 29.)*

# FINDING THE STOLEN GOODS

The **evidence** found by the **CSI**, the analysis of the evidence by the **forensic scientists**, and the interviews conducted with the **witnesses** and **suspects** have all paid off. The chief suspect, the gardener, has finally confessed. There is just one small problem. The gardener has hidden the money and jewels so that an **accomplice** can pick them up for him if he is arrested. You will need to find the stolen goods and return them to the millionaire before you can close the case. Then you will have to find out who the gardener's accomplice is – but that's another case entirely!

## DETECTIVE WORK

You are standing at the tree with the hole in the trunk. Inside, you have found a note for the gardener's accomplice. It gives directions to where the money and jewels are buried.

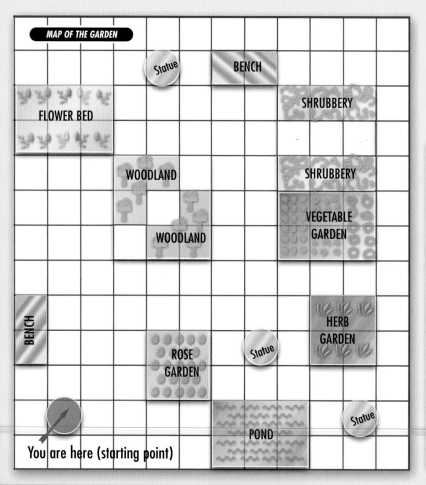

Using the map of the garden and the compass, follow the instructions on the note.

Where in the garden are the stolen goods buried?

**WHERE TO DIG:**

- Go 3 squares north
- 6 squares east
- Diagonally 2 squares southeast
- 2 squares east
- 7 squares north
- 6 squares west
- 1 square south
- Diagonally 2 squares southwest
- 2 squares west
- 3 squares north and dig here!

*(You will find a TIP to help you with this activity on page 29.)*

## FORENSICS FACTS

All living things are made from cells. Inside most cells are instructions for making that person, animal, or plant, stored as a substance called DNA (deoxyribonucleic acid). Forensic scientists can test saliva (spit), skin, hair (if there is some hair root present), and blood, and match the DNA to a suspect. A forensic scientist can find DNA in just a single skin cell. This means that just by touching something such as a doorknob, you are potentially leaving behind your DNA. The blood and hair found at our crime scene could be *DNA tested* to match it to the gardener.

## CHALLENGE QUESTION

The money and jewels are all buried exactly where the note said. Now they can be returned to the millionaire.

If some of the jewels were cut in half so that both halves were the same shape, this is what the jewels would look like. What shape would each jewel be before it was cut in half?

a)

b)

c)

d)

27

# TIPS FOR MATH SUCCESS

## DETECTIVE WORK

**TIP**: Multiplication is the same as doing repeated addition. *For example,* 5 x 3 *is the same as* 5 + 5 + 5.

**Recognizing 2-D shapes:**

An **isoceles triangle** has two sides of equal length.

An **equilateral triangle** has three sides of equal length.

### CHALLENGE QUESTION

The 12x table is:

1 x 12 = 12
2 x 12 = 24
3 x 12 = 36
4 x 12 = 48
5 x 12 = 60
6 x 12 = 72
7 x 12 = 84
8 x 12 = 96
9 x 12 = 108
10 x 12 = 120
11 x 12 = 132
12 x 12 = 144

## CSI WORK

**TIP**: Look carefully at the walls. Where are the door and the French windows? Where are the different items of furniture?

### CHALLENGE QUESTIONS

**Using coordinates:**

To find the coordinates of a point on a grid, you read along the bottom of the grid first, and then up the side of the grid.

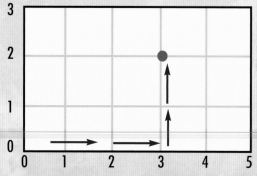

For example, a grid reference of **(3,2)** means **3 steps** along the bottom and then **2 steps** up to find the exact point.

## DETECTIVE WORK

**TIPS**:
- If it takes 1 minute to run 200 yards, then it will take twice as long to run 400 yards – that is, 2 minutes.
- There are 60 seconds in 1 minute.

## CSI WORK

**TIP**: Get yourself organized! Work through this challenge by looking at each part of the picture in turn.

### CHALLENGE QUESTION

**TIP**: An **estimate** is not a guess, but is an answer that we know may be close to what is exactly correct. Being good at estimating helps you to check your math work.

## DETECTIVE WORK

**Using units of measurement:**

**TIP**: When you are given measurements in mixed units, it can be helpful to convert them all to the same unit so that they can be compared.

*For example, 66 inches and 6 feet can be compared as 5½ feet and 6 feet, or as 66 inches and 72 inches.*

(To help with your conversions, see UNITS OF MEASUREMENT on page 29.)

PAGES 18–19

## FORENSIC WORK

### Interpreting a bar graph:

**Bar graphs** have bars that should always be the same width. It is the heights of the bars that allow you to compare things. In a bar graph you need to know what each bar stands for and what the scale is.

*For example, is the scale going up in 1s, 2s, 5s, 10s, 100s, 1,000s, or some other amount?*

PAGES 20–21

## CHALLENGE QUESTIONS

### Using data in a tally chart:

A *tally chart* is a quick way of recording and counting the number or amount of something. One vertical line (l) is marked for "1," two vertical lines (ll) show "2," and so on. The fifth line is then drawn across the first four (卌). Use the 5x table to quickly add when using *tally marks*.

PAGES 24–25

## CHALLENGE QUESTION

You can create your own secret code by giving each letter in the alphabet a number. To make the code hard to crack, you can use the first letter of your name as the number "1" (instead of A) and then continue from there. For example, if your name was George or Grace, your code would look like this:

| 1 | 2 | 3 | 4 | 5 | 6 | 7 |
|---|---|---|---|---|---|---|
| G | H | I | J | K | L | M |
| 8 | 9 | 10 | 11 | 12 | 13 | 14 |
| N | O | P | Q | R | S | T |
| 15 | 16 | 17 | 18 | 19 | 20 | 21 |
| U | V | W | X | Y | Z | A |
| 22 | 23 | 24 | 25 | 26 | | |
| B | C | D | E | F | | |

PAGES 26–27

## DETECTIVE WORK

**TIP**: The line across a square from one corner to the opposite corner is called the diagonal.

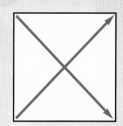

### UNITS OF MEASUREMENT

There are two systems of measurement. The customary system uses inches, feet, miles, ounces, and pounds. The metric system uses centimeters, meters, kilometers, grams, and kilograms.

| METRIC | | CUSTOMARY | |
|---|---|---|---|
| **Length** | | **Length** | |
| 1 millimeter (mm) | | 1 inch (in.) | |
| 1 centimeter (cm) | = 10 mm | 1 foot (ft.) | = 12 in. |
| 1 meter (m) | = 100 cm | 1 yard (yd.) | = 3 ft. |
| 1 kilometer (km) | = 1,000 m | 1 mile | = 1,760 yd. |
| **Weight** | | **Weight** | |
| 1 gram (g) | | 1 ounce (oz.) | |
| 1 kilogram (kg) | = 1,000 g | 1 pound (lb.) | = 16 oz. |
| **Capacity** | | **Capacity** | |
| 1 milliliter (ml) | | 1 fluid ounce (fl. oz.) | |
| 1 liter (l) = 1,000 ml | | 1 pint (pt.) | = 16 fl. oz. |

### Comparing metric and customary measurements:

1 kilometer = 0.62 of a mile
1 kilogram = 2.2 pounds
0.47 liter = 1 pint

## PAGES 6–7

### DETECTIVE WORK

1) $5,500 was stolen.
2) a) The **equilateral triangle** is in box B.
   b) The **isoceles triangle** is in box A.
   c) The **hexagon** is in box B.
   d) The **octagon** is in box C.
3) A) $595 of sapphires were stolen (7 x $85)
   B) $585 of rubies were stolen (9 x $65)
   C) $800 of diamonds were stolen (8 x $100)

### CHALLENGE QUESTION

The code to crack the safe is **12, 24, 36, 48, 72**

## PAGES 8–9

### CSI WORK

Sketch plan B is a correct picture of the room.

### CHALLENGE QUESTIONS

a) The broken glass is outside the French windows.
b) A single hair and fingerprints are in the safe.
c) Fingerprints were found on the table, on the
   fireplace, and in the safe.
d) Muddy footprints were left just inside the
   French windows.
e) A palm print was found on the table.

## PAGES 10–11

### DETECTIVE WORK

1) Five and a half minutes (5 minutes 30 seconds)
2) Eight and a quarter minutes (8 minutes 15 seconds)
3) Seven minutes
4) Five minutes
5) One and a half minutes (1 minute 30 seconds) longer

### CHALLENGE QUESTION

Here are the routes you can take:

| | | |
|---|---|---|
| 1,6,7,3,4 | 4,8,7,2,1 | 4,3,2,6,5 |
| 4,3,7,6,1 | 5,8,3,2,1 | 5,6,2,3,4 |
| 1,2,7,8,4 | 1,2,3,8,5 | |

## PAGES 12–13

### CSI WORK

There are 10 differences between the two pictures.
Dining room B is different from dining room A because:
1. There is a painting next to the cabinet.
2. There is a painting over the fireplace.
3. The light switch by the door is missing.
4. The rug is smaller.
5. An ornament on the top of the cabinet is missing.
6. The painting hiding the safe is straight.
7. French windows have been replaced by regular windows.
8. The chandelier (light) is missing.
9. There is a dog in the room!
10. The bowl of flowers on the table is missing.

### CHALLENGE QUESTION

b) There are 26 fingerprints hidden on pages
12 and 13. How close was your **estimate**?

## PAGES 14–15

### DETECTIVE WORK

1) One person never wears glasses – the jogger.
2) The delivery man does not own white sneakers.
3) The secretary and the chauffeur are the same height.
4) Tallest person is the jogger at 74 inches and the shortest
   person is the maid at 62 inches. The difference is 12
   inches, or 1 foot.
5) The **suspects** are: the secretary, the gardener, the chef,
   the butler, the millionaire's personal trainer, the
chauffeur,         the handyman.

### CHALLENGE QUESTION

Here are the nine different faces that you could make with eyes A.

| | MOUTH | NOSE |
|---|---|---|
| EYES A | A | A |
| | A | B |
| | A | C |
| | B | A |
| | B | B |
| | B | C |
| | C | A |
| | C | B |
| | C | C |

The same number can be made with eyes B or eyes C, and so the
total possible number of different faces is 27.

## PAGES 16–17

### DETECTIVE WORK

The following people had time to commit the crime between 3:40 p.m. and 4:00 p.m.:

- *The personal trainer* – he finished his yoga and weightlifting at 3:30 p.m.
- *The chef* – he finished baking at 3:10 p.m.
- *The gardener* – he finished the cuttings at 3:36 p.m.
- *The butler* – he finished the list of tasks at 3:17 p.m.
- *The chauffeur* – she thinks she returned from the village at about 3:30 p.m.

The following people did not have time to commit the crime:

- *The secretary* – the handyman man saw her go off to the village at 3:30 p.m., and it takes 1 hour 20 minutes to walk to the post office and back. The secretary was busy until 4:50 p.m.
- *The handyman* – all the railings are painted, and so he must have been painting until 4:20 p.m.

### CHALLENGE QUESTION

The chauffeur has remembered that on returning to the mansion she saw the clock at 3:40 p.m.

## PAGES 18–19

### FORENSIC WORK

The butler and the gardener (size 9/10½ inches) and the trainer and the chef (size 10/11 inches) could have made the footprints.

### CHALLENGE QUESTIONS

a) Shoe A: $^{12}/_{36} = ^1/_3$    Shoe B: $^{27}/_{36} = ^3/_4$

   Shoe C: $^5/_{60} = ^1/_{12}$    Shoe D: $^{18}/_{60} = ^3/_{10}$

b) Shoe B: $^3/_4 = 0.75$    Shoe D: $^3/_{10} = 0.3$

## PAGES 20–21

### FORENSIC WORK

The gardener and the butler could still be the **perpetrator**.

| Blood type | Hair color | |
| --- | --- | --- |
| | Brown | Not brown |
| Blood type B | ☺ ☺ | |
| Not blood type B | ☺ | ☺ |

### CHALLENGE QUESTIONS

a) 36 customers  b) 28 customers did not have white hair
c) $^1/_6$ of the total

## PAGES 22–23

### FORENSIC WORK

1)    a) Gardener    b) Gardener   c) Millionaire
      d) Gardener      e) Millionaire

2) Your main **suspect** should be the gardener!

### CHALLENGE QUESTIONS

a) The palm print belongs to the gardener.
b) The gardener should be your main suspect.

## PAGES 24–25

### DETECTIVE WORK

The message reads: GO TO THE TREE SOUTH OF THE GREENHOUSE AND NORTHWEST OF THE TENNIS COURT AND LOOK IN THE HOLE IN THE TRUNK.

## PAGES 26–27

### DETECTIVE WORK

You should be digging in the flower bed to find the stolen goods.

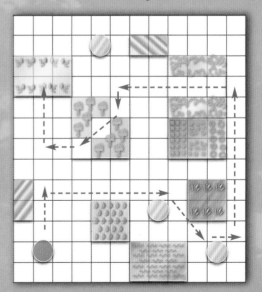

### CHALLENGE QUESTION

a) A **regular hexagon** b) A regular **octagon**
c) A rectangle  d) An **isoceles triangle**

# GLOSSARY

**ACCOMPLICE** A person who works with or helps another person do something. This word is normally used in connection with people who are committing a crime.

**CONTAMINATE** When a substance or an item is mixed in with something else. For example, a hair from a police officer mixing with hairs collected as evidence would mean that the evidence is contaminated.

**CRIME SCENE INVESTIGATOR (CSI)** A specialist investigator who examines the scene of a crime and collects any evidence.

**ELIMINATION PRINTS** Fingerprints taken from the victims of crimes or people who live or work at a crime scene. These prints actually belong at the scene and can therefore be eliminated. Any other prints found have possibly come from a suspect.

**EVIDENCE** Items found at a crime scene, such as fingerprints, hairs, footwear marks, blood, and clothing fibers. Evidence proves a particular person was at a crime scene at some time.

**FINGERPRINTS** Thin, normally invisible, impressions made in sweat of the ridge patterns on fingers.

**FORENSIC SCIENTISTS** Scientists who analyze pieces of evidence recovered from crime scenes.

**PERPETRATOR** A person who commits (perpetrates) a crime.

**STATEMENTS** Verbal accounts of something that has happened. Statements are taken from witnesses, victims, and suspects by a police officer or other investigator. A statement is then put into writing and becomes part of the evidence for that crime.

**SUSPECT** A person who the police believe has committed a crime. The person remains a suspect until they are convicted of the crime, or evidence proves they are innocent.

**VICTIMS** The people who have been affected by a crime – for example, a burglary.

**WITNESSES** The people who see something happen.

## MATH GLOSSARY

**BAR GRAPH** This graph shows information in bars. To read a bar graph you look at the height of the bars against a scale.

**DECIMAL FRACTIONS** We use a counting system involving tens, multiples of ten, and fractions of ten. The decimal point separates whole numbers from decimal fractions. *For example, in the number 672.53, .53 stands for five tenths and three hundredths.*

**EQUILATERAL TRIANGLE** A triangle with all three sides equal in length.

**ESTIMATE** To find a number or amount that is close to an exact answer.

**FRACTION** A fraction is a part of a whole. The bottom number of a fraction (denominator) tells how many parts the whole is divided into. The top number (numerator) tells how many parts of the whole you are referring to. If a shape is divided into four equal parts, each part is ¼ (one-quarter) of the whole.

**HEXAGON** A 2-D (two-dimensional) shape with six angles and six straight sides.

**ISOCELES TRIANGLE** A triangle with two sides equal in length.

**OCTAGON** A 2-D (two-dimensional) shape with eight angles and eight straight sides.

**PRODUCT** The result of multiplying two or more numbers together.

**REGULAR** Used to describe 2-D shapes that have sides that are equal in length and 3-D shapes with faces all the same shape and size.

t=top, b=bottom, c=center, l=left, r=right, OFC=outside front cover, OBC=outside back cover

Alamy: OFC, 1, 6, 8-9c, 12, 13, 16br, 19t, 21 background, 22, OBC.